WYNONA EARP

SEASON ONE YEARBOOK

WYNONNA EARP

SEASON ONE YEARBOOK

Editor: Justin Eisinger and Alonzo Simon • Publisher: Ted Adams
Book Design and Convention Photos: Robbie Robbins • Set and Behind the Scenes Photos: Michelle Faye

For international rights, contact licensing@idwpublishing.com

ISBN: 978-1-63140-893-9

20 19 18 17   1 2 3 4

IDW®
www.IDWPUBLISHING.com

Ted Adams, CEO & Publisher • **Greg Goldstein**, President & COO • **Robbie Robbins**, EVP/Sr. Graphic Artist • **Chris Ryall,** Chief Creative Officer •
David Hedgecock, Editor-in-Chief • **Laurie Windrow**, Senior Vice President of Sales & Marketing • **Matthew Ruzicka**, CPA, Chief Financial Officer •
Lorelei Bunjes, VP of Digital Services • **Jerry Bennington**, VP of New Product Development

Facebook: **facebook.com/idwpublishing** • Twitter: **@idwpublishing** • YouTube: **youtube.com/idwpublishing**
Tumblr: **tumblr.idwpublishing.com** • Instagram: **instagram.com/idwpublishing**

Waverly Earp
Dominique Provost-Chalkley

Agent Dolls
Shamier Anderson

Doc Holliday
Tim Rozon

Nicole Haught

Katherine Barrell

Bobo Del Rey
Michael Eklund

Leavin' on Your Mind

Episode 3

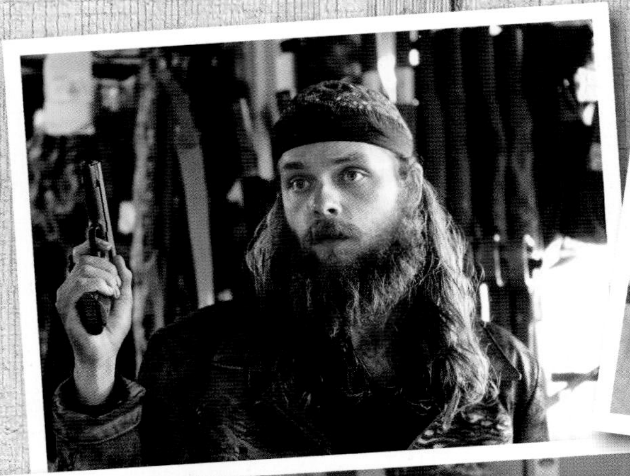

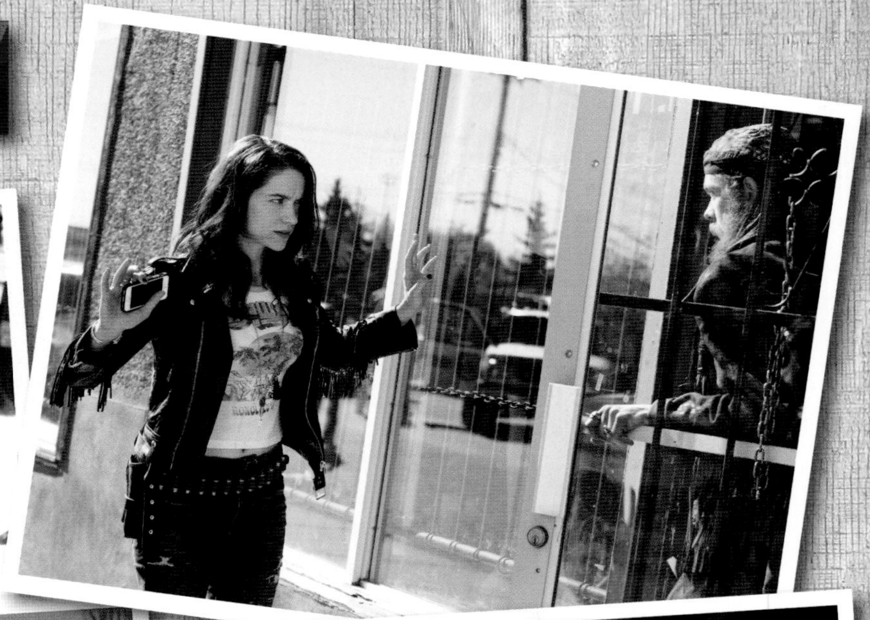

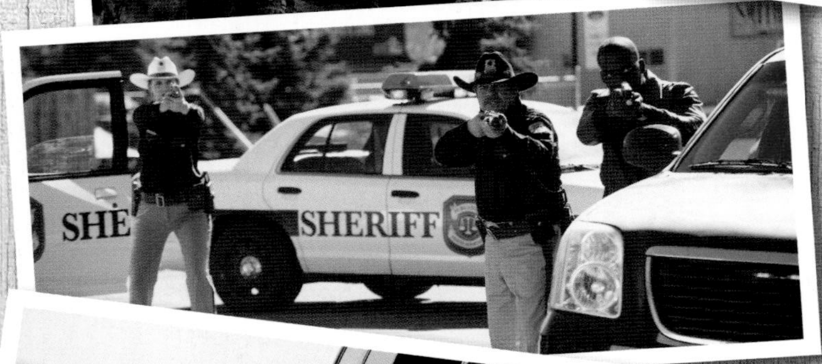

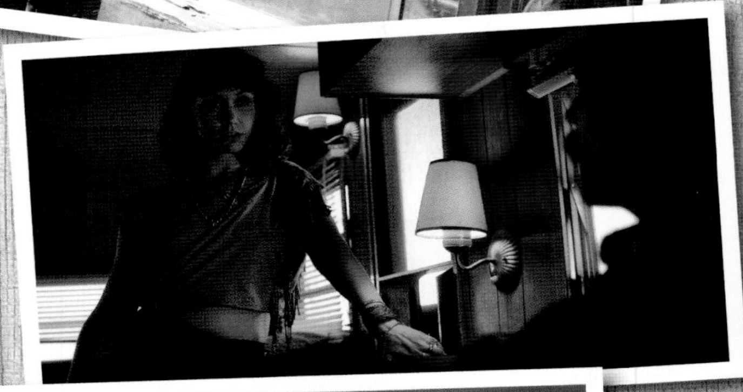

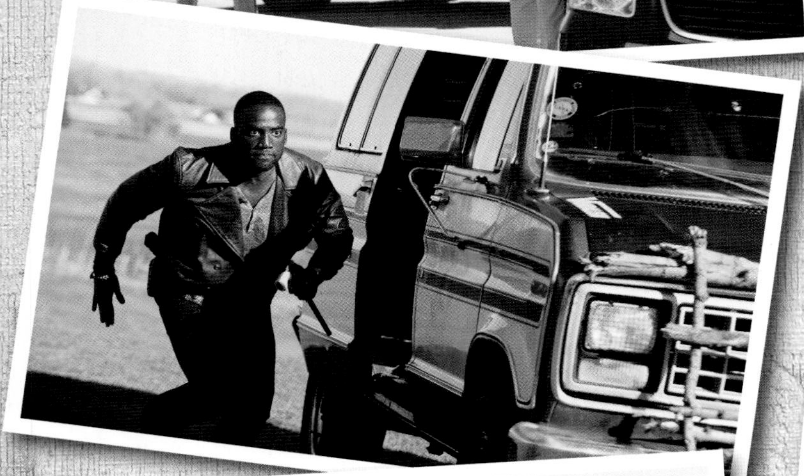

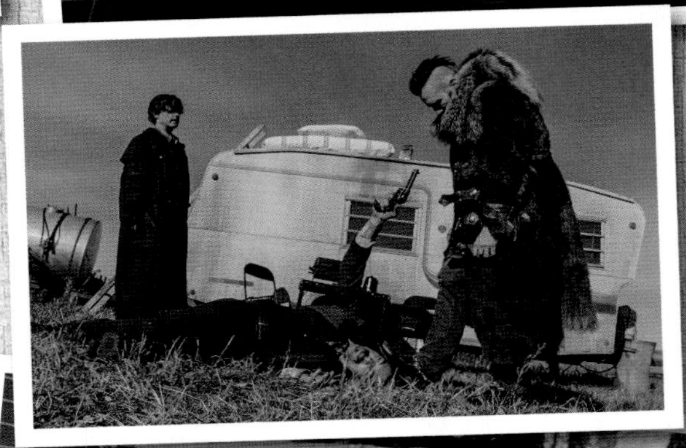

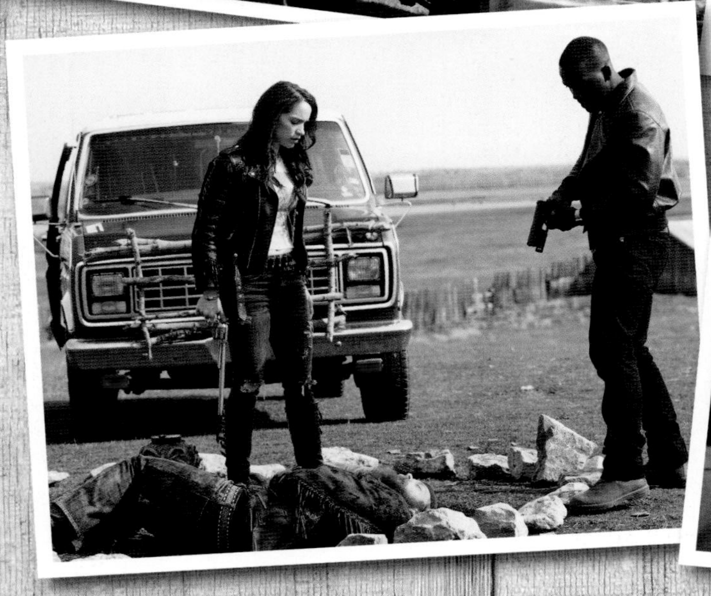

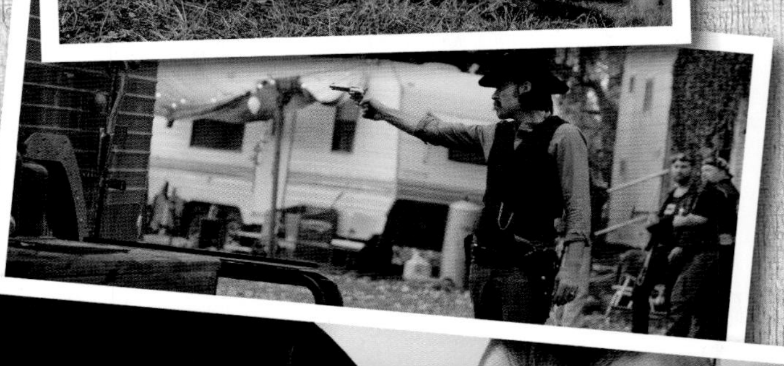

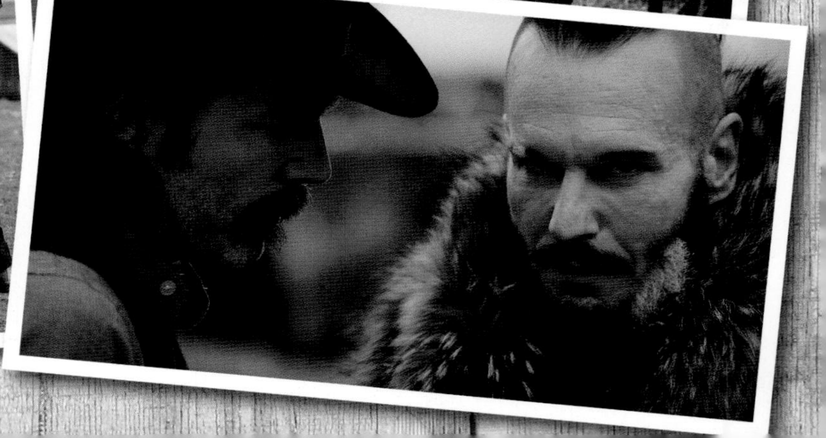

Walking After Midnight
Episode 7

The cast finds out there is a Season two!

Melanie and Dominique celebrate with Emily Andras via Facetime

Shamier and Executive Producer Ted Adams

Executive Producer David Ozer, Tim, and Executive Producer Todd Berger

Beth Smith, Dominique, and Melanie

Wynonna Earp creator Beau Smith, Beth, Ted, and David

Dominique, Melanie, Beau, and Katherine

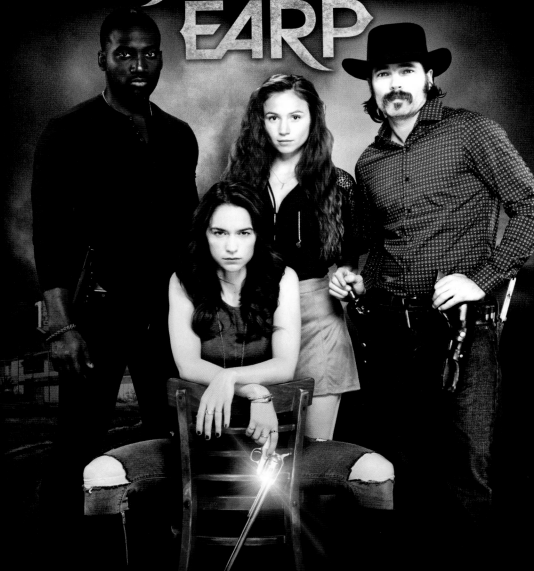

Promotional Poster for Season One

Promotional Brochure for Season One

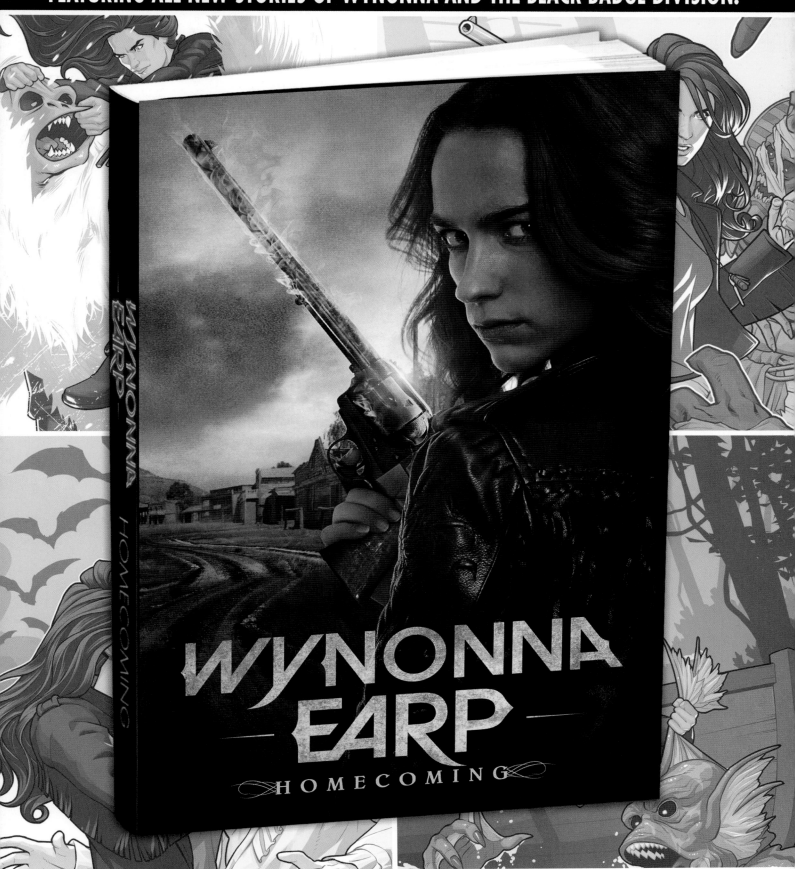

Autographs

Autographs